Dean Blanton

W9-BQV-238

How to Raise Mice, Rats, Hamsters, and Gerbils

A Child's Book of Pet Care

by Sara Bonnett Stein
photographs by Robert Weinreb

Random House   New York

Created by The Open Family Press/Media Projects Incorporated. Design by Mary Gale Moyes.

Library of Congress Cataloging in Publication Data

Stein, Sara Bonnett. How to raise mice, rats, hamsters, and gerbils. (A Child's book of pet care) Includes index. SUMMARY: Discusses the selection and care of various rodents such as mice, rats, hamsters, and gerbils, including hints on choosing or making a cage. 1. Rodents as pets—Juvenile literature. [1. Rodents as pets] I. Title. SF459.R63S73 636'.93'233 76-8138 ISBN 0-394-83224-8 ISBN 0-394-93224-2 lib. bdg.

Manufactured in the United States of America   1 2 3 4 5 6 7 8 9 0

Table of Contents

A Note to Parents

Most parents buy a pet both to satisfy their child's dream and to help him grow a little further. They hope their child will come to see the pet's point of view and care for the animal well. They hope the child will come to share the parents' point of view, too, and stick with his or her responsibilities. But a child doesn't start out thinking that way.

Your child may be thinking that a baby rat will want to be his friend, that he can keep a mouse in his pocket always, that a hamster will sleep in his bed at night, that a gerbil will ride in his toy truck and take a taste of bubble gum.

You may be thinking about the responsibility of cleaning cages, or the tragedy of a hamster lost behind the baseboard, or the annoyance of holes chewed in pockets, or the discomfort of guests who don't like rodents.

Your child is thinking one way, and you another. He has his fantasies; you have your reservations. Because these points of view are so very different, raising a pet rodent can be a disappointing experience—hard on the pet, frustrating to you, and disillusioning to your child. The purpose of this book is to make life with a pet rodent happy for everyone. With some minor but sensible mutual adjustments, you, your child, and your pet can all enjoy each other very much.

The first chapter, "A Pet for a Pocket," introduces children to four pet rodents—the mouse, the rat, the hamster, and the gerbil. It tells what these animals are like in the wild: what homes they make, what foods they eat, what instincts help to keep them safe. It also explains how to set up a cage that imitates a natural home.

Prices for the pets and for the cage and equipment vary. A mouse costs about $1.00, a rat $2.00, a gerbil $3.00. Hamster prices range from $2.00 for a golden hamster to more than $8.00 for a long-haired teddy bear hamster. Commercial cages may cost from $7.00 for the smallest wire cage to $12.00 for a ten-gallon tank cage. A homemade cage costs from $7.00 to $9.00, depending on size. (Directions for making cages are given in this book.) Other equipment, such as a water bottle and a food dish, comes to less than $2.00. Shavings for the cage floor and packaged food will cost about $3.00 a month.

Chapter Two, "Good Food, Clean Homes," explains to children clearly and simply how to care for a pet rodent. Some jobs may require your help. Young children can't cope with a heavy or bulky cage. Some children get upset when shavings spill. They don't want to clean the cage because they can't control the mess. Children may not notice when a cage is dirty, and may not really mind the smell. And most young children can't think in terms of "once a week."

For all these reasons, it is better to set aside a particular time each week for you and your child to clean the cage together. Choose some boring time, when there is really nothing else either of you wants to do. Divide up the job and give your child the simpler tasks—drying the cage, washing the toys, filling the water bottle.

Choose a time for feeding the pet every day, too. Any of the rodents in this book can do without daily feeding if you keep enough dry food in the cage to last several days. But it is much easier for a child to remember to do something every day at a certain time (just before his or her dinner, for instance) than to check the food on an irregular basis. Keep the food right next to the cage, too, so the job is not too complicated.

Your child may want to keep his pet in his own room. But the two of you are not often in the room together. When you notice the cage is dirty, your child isn't there to remind. And when you do remind him, neither of you is near the cage. He finds it easier to put his job off, you find it easier to nag, and the pet ends up neglected.

Many families discover there is less reminding—and less nagging—when a pet is kept in a social part of the home such as the kitchen or playroom. There, care of the pet can be a cooperative effort. Others in the family can offer help as it is needed, and compliments, and a bit of cheese from a sandwich. Such sharing does not damage a child's sense of responsibility, and the routine care of the pet becomes a happy part of living together as a family.

Chapter Three, "Playtime," suggests chummy things that children can do with pets and toys they can make. Children perceive animals as being much like themselves. You may find your child giving his or her pet a bath. He may set up a tea party or expect his pet to love having a ribbon on its tail. It is not necessary or even possible to disenchant children of those notions. Instead, in this chapter they can learn about humanlike entertainments that will satisfy them but not harm the pet.

The last chapter, "A Beginning and an End," is about birth and death. You may wish to breed your child's pet. Watching a mother animal care for a litter of babies is a lovely and natural experience for children. Of course, things can go wrong. Malformed or sickly babies fail to trigger maternal behavior in a rodent. Such an infant is treated as "non-baby," and may be eaten. Lack of a decent nest and malnutrition may have the same effect on maternal instincts. Luckily, attacking a baby is rare and can almost always be prevented by feeding the mother a varied diet and providing her with good nest materials.

Occasionally a pet escapes. If an escaped pet is never found, there will be questions to answer. Did he go back to his mommy? Will he be sad all alone? Is he dead? If you never find a pet's body (or smell it) the pet is probably not dead. Many escaped pets can learn to live in the wild. If you find the animal dead, tell your child the truth.

Fatal accidents commonly befall these small rodents. Unless a cage top is firmly secured, cats can open it and attack the rodent. A fall from a table or a child's hands can cause a concussion. Even with the best of care, pet rodents do not live for more than several years. So the last pages of this book tell how to hold a funeral for a pet, in honor of the little life that has ended.

Chapter One
A Pet for a Pocket

This book is about four small furry animals: the mouse, the rat, the hamster, and the gerbil. They all belong to the group of animals called rodents. Each of them can be tamed. Each can be held and petted. They hold their food in their front paws when they eat. They wash their paws afterwards, and wipe their faces and whiskers. They can sit up and beg for food. They can climb and hide and play with toys. You can give them a ride in your pocket.

Rodents all have long front teeth. Your teeth stop growing when they are big enough. But a rodent's front teeth never stop growing. Rodents eat hard foods—nuts and grains and bark. Gnawing on these hard foods wears their teeth down. If the rodents' teeth didn't keep growing, they would wear down too short.

Mice, rats, hamsters, and gerbils don't understand about their teeth. But a feeling inside them makes them want to gnaw on hard things. This feeling is called an instinct. The gnawing instinct makes pet rodents want to chew on anything they find.

Your pet will do many things because his instincts make him. If your pet lived wild in the woods, foxes and owls would chase him and try to eat him. He would be too small to fight back. He would try to hide instead. He would scurry under a rock. He would chew a hole in the wall of a house and hide inside. Or he would dig tunnels and rooms under the ground. When he found a safe place to live, he would build a nest there to make it comfortable.

A pet rodent wants to hide, too. He wants to dig. He wants to build a nest. He has never seen a fox or an owl, but he feels safer if he can live in a small, dark place. Digging and hiding and building nests are instincts, too.

Rodents usually sleep during the day and move around all night. When it is time to wake up and look for dinner, they come out of their hiding places. They are not scared all the time. They want to explore new places and new things. If they see an old tin can, they climb into it. Maybe the can could be a

new hiding place. They sniff it. They nibble the edge. Maybe the can has something good to eat on it. This instinct to explore helps wild rodents to find enough food. It helps them to find places to hide from hungry animals, too.

But your rodent is a pet. He lives in a cage. When he feels like gnawing, he can't go out and find a stick to chew on. When he feels like digging, he can't make a new tunnel in the soft ground outdoors. Where can he hide? What can he explore? His instincts make him want to do these things. He needs you to help him. You can give him things to chew, and stuff to dig in, and places to hide. You can take him out of his cage and let him explore. You can feed him. You can make him happy. That is how you and your pet can be friends.

Mice

Some people like mice best of all the rodents because they are the tiniest. There are brown mice and black ones, blond mice and white ones. There are even spotted mice.

A mouse is always busy. He stands up on his hind legs to sniff the air. He pokes his nose into any small place to see if he can hide there. He runs and climbs. A mouse will even walk along the edge of a box like a tightrope walker. His tail moves from side to side to balance him.

A mouse uses his whiskers to find out things. The whiskers stick out in front and on both sides of his head. If a mouse is about to bump into something, his whiskers warn him first. If a hole is too small for him to fit into, his whiskers tell him so.

Watch how a mouse moves. He leans forward. He sniffs. He wiggles his whiskers. Then he runs. He stops. He sniffs and wiggles his whiskers. Then he runs again.

The only time a mouse stops moving is when he curls up into a ball and falls asleep. He likes to sleep in the daytime. He likes to be busy all night. But your mouse will not mind when you wake him up to play with him.

You can tame a mouse so he is used to you. When he is used to your smell and your hands, he will not nip you. But you can never make a mouse really calm. Every mouse is busy and nervous and in a hurry. When you take a mouse out of his cage, you have to watch him every minute. While you are not looking, he will sniff, wiggle his whiskers, and run and hide. That is how pet mice get lost.

A mouse keeps his body very clean. He licks himself all over. He wets his paws and then washes his whiskers with them. A mouse washes behind his ears with his paws, too. He uses his nails to comb his fur. He even picks up his tail and gives it a good licking.

The biggest trouble with a mouse is that his cage gets smelly. His urine smells very strong. Most people who keep mice have to clean the cage twice a week so that it doesn't smell bad.

Rats

Wild rats are scary animals. But pet rats are not like wild ones at all. Pet rats are much smaller than wild rats. Most of them are white. Hooded rats have a black head and a black stripe on their backs. Sometimes you can find a pet rat that is all shiny black. Pet rats are very tame. A rat won't bite even if you give him a bath or dress him in a party hat.

A rat is interested in your company. He loves to come out of his cage. You can wake him up in the daytime. He won't mind. Carry him around. Let him sit on your shoulder. He may wash himself there. Let him play on the floor. Unless a rat is very young, he will not run away and hide. If you can't find your rat for a while, he is probably just exploring.

Rats are smarter than mice, hamsters, and gerbils. You can train a rat to come when you whistle. He will sit up and beg for a snack. A rat can hold onto a string with his paws and swing from it. He can use his heavy tail to balance him when he walks along a stick.

But not everything about rats is good. They are not tiny. They can't fit inside your two hands. A male rat has a funny smell, though a female doesn't. Rats chew on things as all rodents do. Their teeth are large. They can make holes in almost anything.

The worst problem is that many people don't like rats. They are scared of them. They don't like the rat's naked tail. They get upset when they see a rat. So you will not be able to show off your rat to everyone.

Hooded rat

Hamsters

Hamsters' tails are so short you can hardly see them. Their behinds are plump and round. Hamsters come in pretty colors. Their fur is especially soft. One kind of hamster is called a teddy bear hamster. His fur is so fluffy he looks like a stuffed toy.

Hamsters love to carry food around and hide it. A hamster picks up a piece of food with his paws. He stuffs it into his mouth, but he may not swallow it. Inside his cheeks are large pouches. A hamster can stuff food into his pouches until he looks as if he has mumps. Later on, he puts the food in a hiding place. When he is hungry, he finds the food and eats it up.

Wild hamsters hide food because they are saving it for winter. They are making sure they will have enough to eat during cold weather. Even though you always feed a pet hamster enough food, his instinct will make him hide some. He will hide seeds, and fresh food such as lettuce and apples.

Fresh food gets rotten after a day or so. Rotten food is not healthy. You will have to be a little mean to your hamster. You will have to find his hiding places and take his rotten food away from him.

Hamsters are easy to tame if you buy them when they are babies. But they nip a lot—more than mice, rats, and gerbils. A hamster is grouchy when you wake him up. He is grumpy while he is eating. He is annoyed if you bother him while he is fixing up his nest. He doesn't like you to squeeze him in your hand. He might nip you at any of these times. And he might nip you if he sees your hand coming to pick

him up—especially when he is in a corner of his cage. You have to pick a hamster up from behind. And you have to let him alone while he eats or builds his nest. If you wake up your hamster, let him eat some dinner before you take him out to play. Sometimes he won't want to wake up at all in the daytime.

Hamsters get lost easily. They can squeeze through very small spaces. When they hide, they don't like to come out again. Hamsters can't climb like rats and mice. They don't see well in the daytime either. They can fall from your hands or tumble off tables. You have to protect a hamster more than other rodents.

Hamsters need to run a lot. The safest way to let a hamster run is on an exercise wheel inside his cage.

Teddy bear hamster (left) and golden hamster

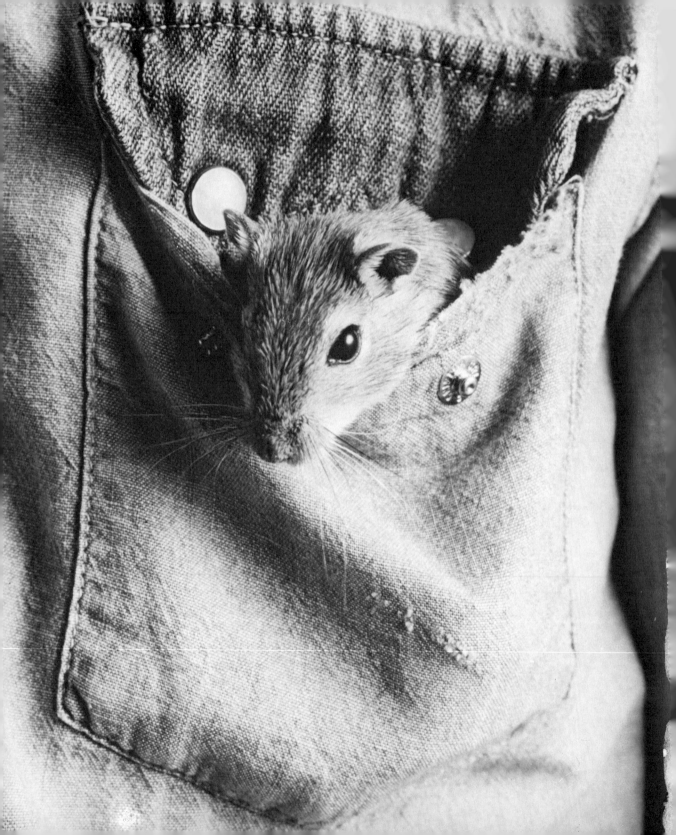

Gerbils

Gerbils come in only one color, a nice plain brown that is lighter on the belly. Their fur is oily, so they do not look or feel as fluffy as hamsters. Their tails are furry and have a tassel at the end.

Gerbils are desert animals. They don't need a lot of water. They make only a few drops of urine every day. Their cage doesn't get dirty or smelly. You need to wash it only once a month. Gerbils are the easiest rodents to take care of.

In the desert, gerbils dig tunnels to live in. Their instinct to dig is very strong. A gerbil will try to dig a tunnel in his cage. Even though he can never make a hole in the metal floor, he will dig and dig all night.

Gerbils are easy to tame. They are not as nervous as mice. They hardly ever bite. They don't get lost as often as hamsters and mice. They don't run and hide as quickly as mice. They can't squeeze into small places as well as hamsters. If you forget to watch a gerbil for a minute, he may still be around when you remember to look for him.

Cages

Before you buy a pet, you have to make a home ready for him. A rodent home is a cage made of metal or glass or plastic that is too tough to chew up. You put wood shavings on the floor of the cage to make it comfortable. The photographs on these pages show the different kinds of rodent cages you can buy at a pet store. Also shown is a cage that you can make at home. Directions for making it are on the next pages.

Metal wire cages have a pan in the bottom that pulls out like a drawer. You pull the pan out to clean it. The edges of the pan might be sharp. They can cut your fingers. Wire cages also have a small door. It is hard to reach your hands in through the door to take your pet out. You may have to wait for him to come out by himself. Some wire cages come with an exercise wheel, and some don't. The wire cage shown here is a good size for a rat, a hamster, or a gerbil. It measures 16 inches by 8 inches. If you want your pet to have babies, get a cage 20 inches by 12 inches. Even the smallest wire cage has bars too far apart to hold a young mouse. He could slip right through and escape. The only safe kind of wire cage for mice is the kind you make yourself.

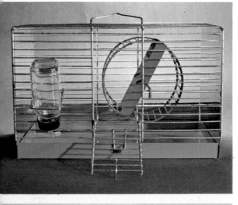

A fish tank with glass sides is a good cage for mice, too. And a tank is the best cage for a gerbil. When a gerbil digs, he kicks his wood shavings around. The shavings come out of a wire cage and make a mess. The shavings can't be kicked out of a tank. A five-and-a-half-gallon tank is big enough for

a mouse, a gerbil, or a hamster. A ten-gallon tank is better for a rat. Buy a ten-gallon tank if you want your pet to have babies. Pet stores sell wire tops to fit both these tanks. When you want to play with your pet, you can easily take the top off to reach him. But a tank cage is heavy. You may need help to clean it.

The fancy plastic cage with tunnels and rooms is made for hamsters. Gerbils like it too. It is called Habitrail. You can buy a small Habitrail first, then buy more pieces later to make it fancier. The bottom box is the part you clean. The Habitrail cage does not always work very well. The pieces may come apart when you don't want them to. Or they may not come apart when you need them to.

The easiest cage to take care of is a homemade one. The bottom and top are aluminum cake pans. The sides are a kind of wire screening called hardware cloth. A cake pan is deep enough to hold lots of wood shavings. The bottom pan is easy to clean. The top pan comes off so you can reach your pet easily. A small cake-pan cage is good for a mouse or a gerbil. A bigger cake-pan cage is good for a hamster or a rat. Make the big size if your pet will have babies. A still bigger cage can be made out of two roasting pans. Even two grown-up rats could live in it. A roasting-pan cage is big enough to hold an exercise wheel, too.

Trimming the hardware cloth

Fitting the first side

Creasing the cloth

A Homemade Cage

A cake-pan cage is too hard for you to make by yourself. But you can help your parents measure the hardware cloth and bend it. You can hold things straight and hand them tools. The job takes about one hour.

For a small cage you need:

> two aluminum cake pans,
> 9 inches by 9 inches
>
> ¼-inch mesh hardware cloth,
> 38 inches by 11 inches
>
> 3 feet of bendable wire

For a large cage you need:

> two aluminum cake pans,
> 9 inches by 13 inches
>
> ¼-inch mesh hardware cloth,
> 46 inches by 14 inches
>
> 3 feet of bendable wire

For a roasting-pan cage you need:

> two aluminum roasting pans,
> 12 inches by 18 inches
>
> ½-inch mesh hardware cloth,
> 62 inches by 15 inches
>
> 3 feet of bendable wire

Hardware stores sell all these materials. Before you buy the hardware cloth, make sure the mesh squares are straight. If the squares are slanted, don't buy that piece of hardware cloth. Slanted hardware cloth makes a jiggly cage.

Use wire shears to trim the cloth if the hardware store hasn't cut it to the exact size. Cut the sharp wire points off the edges.

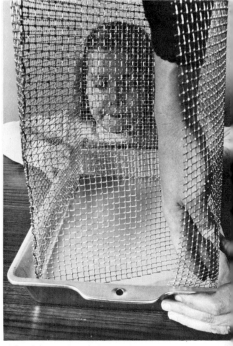

Marking the last crease

To make the cage, you have to crease the hardware cloth so that it fits snugly into the cake pans. Stand the cloth in a pan. Press one end tightly into a corner. Mark off the first side of the cage by pinching the cloth where it meets the next corner of the pan. Take the cloth out. Starting at the pinched point, crease the cloth from bottom to top. Creasing the cloth over the edge of a table keeps your fold straight.

Crease the cloth at the other corners in the same way. When you get back to the first corner, the cloth should overlap it by two or more inches. Trim the overlap to two inches. Crease the cloth at this corner, too.

Check that your creases are in the right places. The wire sides should reach all the way to the bottom of the pan. Then weave the bendable wire through the overlap to hold the first corner closed. Stand the cloth in the bottom pan, put the other pan on top, and you are finished.

Weaving wire through the overlap

Other Equipment

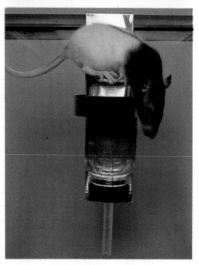

You need wood shavings, nest material, a water bottle, and a food dish to make your pet's cage into a home. You might also want to give him an exercise wheel. You can buy everything but nest material at a pet store. Buy some food while you are there, too.

Shavings keep a cage dry and comfortable. They help keep a cage from smelling, too. Green shavings are made from pine wood colored green with chlorophyll. Chlorophyll stops some smells. White shavings are made of plain pine wood. Reddish shavings are made of cedar wood. Cedar has a strong smell that covers up the smell of mice. But some rodents are allergic to cedar. If your pet sneezes a lot in cedar shavings, you'll have to buy another kind.

Your pet needs nest material so he can build a sleeping nest. Look around the house for old rags or paper towels. Wood shavings won't work for a nest. They don't stick together well enough. On page 37 is a list of other materials that are good for nests.

A water bottle is the easiest way to give water to your pet. The water stays clean. It doesn't spill. The bottle holds enough water to last several days. Your pet licks just the amount he needs from the bottom of the spout.

The cheapest water bottles have a glass spout. The spout jiggles and leaks. A rodent can bite through the glass and cut his mouth on it. The best

22

water bottles have a metal spout with a metal ball inside that prevents leaking. A company called Oasis makes this kind of bottle for parakeets, but it is good for rodents, too.

A water bottle is attached to a cage with a holder called a bracket. Wire cages come with the bracket already on the cage. The bottle slides into the bracket. If you made your own cage, you have to make your own bracket. Bend six inches of wire into a bracket like the one in this picture. A tank cage needs a different kind of bracket to hold the water bottle. It is made of flat metal.

A food dish keeps food clean. The dish should be heavy and deep so your pet can't tip it over as he eats. Buy a dish made of china so your pet can't chew it up. Don't forget to buy food. You will have to have dinner ready for your pet when you bring him home. Pages 28 to 30 tell you the kinds of food that are best for each animal.

If your cage doesn't have an exercise wheel, you may want to buy one. Hamsters especially need a wheel to run in. The best kind attaches to the cage wires. There is also a kind that stands up on its own base. It goes on the floor of your pet's cage. Test the wheel before you buy it. Sometimes a wheel is crooked and doesn't spin well. Be sure the wheel fits in your cage, too. It shouldn't take up more than a third of the space inside the cage.

Making a Home

Now you have everything you need to make a home for your pet. Here is how you get his home ready.

The cage may be dusty. Wipe it out with a damp sponge and dry it well. Put wood shavings into the bottom. The shavings should be one inch deep. Clean up any shavings that spill.

Rinse out the food dish and dry it. Fill it up with the food you bought at the pet store. Put the dish in a front corner of the cage, where it won't be in your pet's way.

Rinse out the water bottle. Fill it with water and screw the top on tightly. Turn the bottle over to see if the spout is working. If water drips from the spout, tighten the top more. Rub your finger against the bottom of the spout. If no water comes out, loosen the top a little. When the spout works well, attach the bottle to the cage.

The water bottle hangs on the outside of a wire cage or homemade cage. First stick the spout in through the wire. (If the spout won't fit through a mesh square, make the square bigger by prying it with a screwdriver.) Then lower the bracket over the bottle. If you have a tank, the bottle goes inside. Hang the bracket from the top edge and just lower the bottle into it.

If you are adding an exercise wheel to the cage, place it to one side.

Now put in paper or rags for a nest. The bunch of nest material should be about as big as a baseball.

Don't try to make the nest yourself. Your pet will want to build his own. When he moves into his new home, he will choose a dark corner for his nest. If the cage sits against a wall, the nest will be in a back corner. Your pet will build his nest the first night. He will chew and tear the paper and cloth. He will shape it with his paws. In the morning the new nest will be finished. And that is where he will always sleep.

The New Baby

Buy your pet when he is still a baby. A rodent can leave his mother as soon as he can eat grown-up food. Try to find a baby who has just stopped drinking his mother's milk. He should be four or five weeks old. At that age, he is not afraid of people. He does not run fast yet. He is not grouchy or nippy. And he is so cute the rest of your family will like him, too.

Tell the clerk in the pet store which baby you like best. Ask if it is a boy or a girl. The boy has testicles below his tail. They look like a furry lump. They are still small, but the clerk can usually see them. If you want your pet to have babies, just buy a girl now. You can buy or borrow a mate for her when she is grown up.

The pet store clerk will put your baby rodent into a cardboard box. You might feel like opening the box before you get home. You might feel like holding your pet right away. Opening the box now is

not a good idea. The baby will be upset. He may try to escape. Wait until you are ready to put the baby in his new home. Then open the box.

Many people pick up a baby mouse, rat, or gerbil by his tail. It does not hurt him. You can't pick up a hamster that way. His tail is too short. Any baby rodent will be more comfortable if you pick him up by putting your hand under him. Move your hand slowly. Scoop the baby up from behind. Don't close your hand or squeeze him. He will not try to jump or run if you are gentle. Open the door of his cage and put the baby in. Close the door right away.

Watch your baby rodent explore the home you fixed for him. He probably will sniff around the cage first. He may taste his dinner. He may try the water bottle. He may comb his hair and wash his face. He may even start to make his nest. Exploring, getting used to his cage, and fixing his bed will help the baby feel calm again. In an hour, you can take him out of his cage and play with him in your hands.

Chapter Two
Good Food, Clean Homes

Feeding

Rodents eat many meals a day. They move quickly. Their hearts beat fast. Their bodies use a lot of food. You have to be sure a mouse, a rat, a hamster, or a gerbil always has food in his cage.

Pet rodents eat mostly seeds. They eat the seeds of grasses such as oats and wheat. They eat the seeds of flowers such as sunflowers. And they eat the seeds of trees—nuts and softer seeds. When you buy rodent food, you can see different kinds of seeds in it. You might also see brown bits that look a little like pills. They are called lab chow. Lab chow is made of seeds and dry grass that have been ground up and pressed into pills.

Seeds and lab chow are hard foods. They keep a rodent's front teeth from growing too long. As a rodent gnaws on them, his teeth wear down. Your pet will always need to have hard foods to gnaw on.

When a rodent lives in the wild, he can eat what he wants. His body tells him when he needs some vegetables, when he needs some fat, and when he needs some seeds. When a rodent lives in a cage, he can eat only what you give him. Pet stores sell a special food for hamsters and another special food for gerbils. They don't usually sell special food for mice or for rats. Buy gerbil food instead. Boxed rodent foods contain seeds such as corn, millet, milo, wheat, oats, and sunflower seed. Hamster food sometimes has dried bits of vegetables in it, too. Boxed food may also have lab chow in it.

None of the boxed foods have everything in them that your pet needs. You have to give your pet plenty of snacks, too. The snacks are often the same foods that keep you healthy: fresh washed vegetables, apples, cereal, cheese, hard-boiled eggs, and even meat. Your pet's body will tell him which of these foods to eat.

The pictures on the next page show about how much food each pet rodent can eat in one day. The pictures also show some of the snacks you should give your pet. Most of the food shown is hard seeds and lab chow. The rest is snacks.

Gerbils stick to dry foods more than other pet rodents. Popcorn is made of corn seeds, so it makes a healthy snack for a gerbil. Raw oatmeal would be fine too. Some gerbils love potato chips. Gerbils will eat a little lettuce or raw spinach, a bit of tomato, a slice of raw carrot. And sometimes a gerbil eats snacks of cheese or hard-boiled egg.

Hamsters need more fresh vegetables than most rodents. They enjoy lettuce and string beans and bits of fruit such as this chunk of apple. If a hamster eats too many fresh foods at once, he can get diarrhea. Start with tiny snacks until his body gets used to fresh foods. This hamster likes to open peanuts. The big seeds are sunflower seeds. The hamster loves them, but they are fattening, and he can't have too many.

Rats eat just about everything. The chicken bone is good for this rat to chew on. He would like it even better if it had some meat left on it. He loves cheese. A grape is too big for a mouse to hold in his paws, but this rat can easily hold a grape to munch on it. Spinach is a good vegetable for him. Its dark green color tells you it has lots of vitamins and minerals. A rat's teeth are strong enough to open hard-shelled nuts.

Mice really do like cheese. They like anything that has lots of fat in it. That's why mice love peanut butter and bacon, too. But if you see your pet is getting fat, you have to make these snacks smaller. Mice enjoy meat, so a tiny bit of hamburger or raw chicken would be a nice snack. Keep the snack small so no meat is left over to rot in the cage.

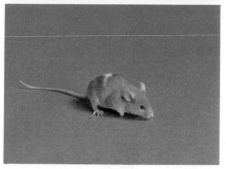

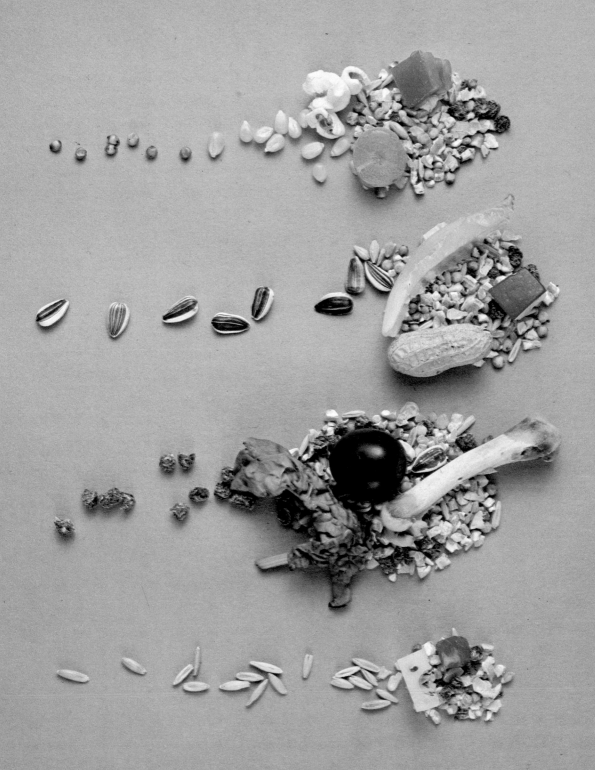

Daily Care

There are some things you should do every day to take care of a mouse, a rat, a hamster, or a gerbil.

Take the food dish out of the cage. (Don't forget to close the cage door.) Empty the dish into the garbage can. Then fill it up again with seeds and lab chow. When you first look at the food dish, you may think it is still full of seeds. You may think you don't need to feed your pet today. But seeds can fool you. If you look carefully, the dish is probably full of empty shells—just as the dish in this picture is. Your pet has eaten the insides and dropped the shells back into his dish.

Check to see if the water bottle needs more water. Bottles work best if they are at least half full.

Check that the water is coming through the spout of the bottle. Put your finger on the end of the spout and rub it back and forth. If you finger stays dry, the bottle is not working. If your pet chews on the spout a lot, that is another sign that the bottle isn't working. He is trying to get at the water, but it is not dripping through. Loosen the top a little, shake the bottle, and rub your finger on the spout to get the water started again.

Check the shavings under the water bottle spout. If they are wet, the spout has been leaking. Tighten the bottle top hard to stop the leak.

Poke around in the shavings now and try to find any leftover snacks. Hamsters are especially likely to hide their snacks. Leftover food, such as old cheese and vegetables, is not good for your pet.

Take it out and throw it away. You can leave a bone in the cage. Your pet has probably cleaned off the meat. The dry bone will not rot as vegetables do. Dry foods such as seeds and lab chow are safe to leave, too.

When you finish working in the cage, take your pet out for a while. Now is a good time to play with him. While you were fussing with his cage, he has had a chance to wake up. He has become interested in what is going on. Even a grumpy hamster is usually ready to keep you company.

If you handle your rodent every day, he will stay tame. Let him walk from one hand to the other. Let him look inside your pockets. Let him sit on your shoulder or peek out through your hair. A few minutes of handling are enough to keep your pet used to you. If you are busy now, put him back in his home. If you want to play some more, pages 36 to 39 tell you about toys, games, and playgrounds.

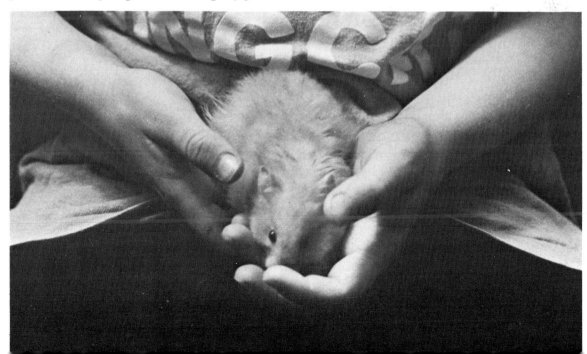

Cage Cleaning

Why does a cage have to be cleaned when it may not look dirty and may not smell? Urine soaks into the shavings. It makes the pet's skin sore. Germs from droppings and old food can make your pet sick.

A mouse's cage should be cleaned once a week. But it if gets smelly, you may want to clean it twice a week.

A rat's cage or a hamster's cage should be cleaned once a week.

A gerbil's cage has to be cleaned only once a month.

Put your pet in a container before you clean his cage. A jar or a coffee can will do for mice, hamsters, and gerbils. A bucket would be better for a rat. An empty bathtub is a safe container for any of these pets. Close the drain first and pull the shower curtain to the outside of the tub. The sides of all these containers are too slippery to climb, and too high to jump over.

Move the cage to a place where spilled shavings won't be hard to clean up. The kitchen might be the best spot. The kitchen sink is a good place to wash the cage, too. Take the food dish, the water bottle, and any toys out of the cage. Save the nest if it is not too dirty. Or save a piece of it. It is your pet's own bed. He doesn't like to lose all of it. Dump the shavings into a big paper bag. Some will spill. Clean them up now before they get spread about.

Wash the bottom tray or pan of the cage with

soap or detergent and hot water. If you have a tank cage, wash out the whole tank. Shavings can stick in the corners of any cage. Use a brush or sink spray to get them out. Wash the toys, the food dish, and the water bottle, too. A bottle brush is good for washing the water bottle. Rinse everything very well. Your pet should not get soap in his mouth when he chews on things. Dry everything, too.

When the dry cage is back together, put in fresh shavings. Put what is left of the nest back where your pet keeps it. Add a rag or a paper towel so your pet can fix the nest up again. Fill the water bottle and attach it to the cage. Fill the food dish and put it back in its usual corner. Maybe now you would like to add a treat: a bone or a twig to chew on, some grass to add to the nest, or a new toy. When the cage looks homey, put your pet back in. Soon he will fix his nest and be very happy.

Once in a while, you might feel like giving your pet a washing, too. Most rodents don't mind water if it is warm. They don't like hot or cold water. Soap is not good for them, so don't give your pet a shampoo. After his bath, dry him gently with a towel.

Chapter Three
Playtime

Presents for Your Pet

You play with toys. Your pet rodent does, too. His toys are different from your toys. But the ways he has fun are not so different from yours. A rodent has fun hiding and peeking. Maybe you do that sometimes. A rodent likes to chew. Maybe you chew on gum or nibble pencils. A rodent loves to build a soft nest. Maybe you build houses with soft blankets and pillows. A rodent has fun exploring new places. He likes playgrounds just as you do.

A rodent wants to hide and chew and build and explore because these are his instincts. How can he do these things in a bare cage? He can chew on his wire cage. But chewing on wire is no fun. If he has no nest materials, he will try to make a nest of shavings. But it will fall apart. He will try to hide in a corner. But everyone can see him. He has no place to hide. And he has no place to explore.

Your pet will be happier if you give him toys to play with in his cage. He will be happier if you take him out to play in a rodent playground sometimes. And you will have a good time watching him enjoy his presents.

You can find chewing toys in your house and outside. Your pet will gnaw on scraps of wood and pieces of dowel sticks, such as a chunk of an old mop handle. Green twigs from trees are good. Your pet might like to eat the bark. Give him a chicken bone or a chop bone. Rats and mice will eat the scraps of meat from bones. Hamsters and gerbils might not eat the meat. Give them cleaned bones to gnaw on. Your pet might eat the bone, too. It is good food for him. Rodents chew the rounded metal edges of small cans, such as frozen juice cans. They like the soft plastic tops of coffee cans, too.

You can give your pet nest materials that are more interesting than paper towels and rags. Give him a present of ribbons, a torn sock, a worn-out knitted mitten, or a ragged washcloth. He would have fun with knitting yarn, too. He might also like cotton balls or dried grass clippings.

A new place to hide is a wonderful present for your pet. Take both ends off a small can such as a tomato paste or frozen juice can. It can be a hiding tunnel. A rat needs a bigger can. A toilet paper tube can be a tunnel, too. But your pet will soon chew it up and need a new one. Rodents will hide inside socks and mittens. Then they will chew them up and add them to the nest. A small cardboard box with the top left on is a good hiding place. Your pet will make his own door, but he may not mind if you tear or cut one for him. He might build his nest inside the box. He will chew on it, too.

A plastic container lasts longer than a box. Margarine and other foods come in soft plastic containers. Use colored or white ones, not clear ones. Keep the top on. Cut a door or let your pet chew one himself. Turn the container upside down in your pet's cage.

A Playground

The picture on this page shows ways you can put together sticks, wood scraps, and string to make a playground for your pet. (You can also use cans, cardboard tubes, boxes, and chains.) The playground has places to climb and hide. It has a seesaw and a swing. It has a picnic table, too.

Children made this playground themselves. They got the wood dowels (wooden sticks) at the hardware store. They found the string and scraps of wood at home. They used white glue to hold the pieces together. They sprayed the pieces with enamel paint. The different toys are just arranged on the floor or on a table to make the playground.

A playground is a good place for a pet to learn tricks. Rats learn tricks best. Whenever you take your rat out to play, put his favorite snack in the same place in his playground. He will learn to look there and find it. If you can, whistle when you give him the food. He can learn to come when you whistle, but you must do it many times.

Rats and mice are good at balancing, too. Mice can walk across the thin stick in this picture. Rats can hang from a string by their front paws.

All the rodents in this book can learn to sit up and beg. Hold a bit of favorite food above your pet's nose. If he is hungry, he will sit up to take the food from your fingers.

Snapshots

People often take pictures of their dog or cat. But they think it is too hard to take pictures of a pocket-sized pet. A mouse runs around so much. A hamster keeps hiding. And a picture of a pet inside a cage isn't very interesting.

These snapshots were taken by children. They will give you some ideas of how to make your pet do cute things. They will show you how to make your pet sit still so you can take his picture.

The gerbil is in a hiding place. You could put your pet in a toilet paper tube, too, or in a pocket or a can. Get the camera ready to take a picture of the hiding place. Sooner or later the gerbil will stick his head out. Then you can snap the picture.

The rat in the toy truck is not trying to drive. His owner put peanut butter on the steering wheel. The rat is interested in the peanut butter. He stays in the truck to eat it. There is plenty of time to take his picture.

The mouse is sitting on top of a milk bottle. He doesn't want to jump. The bottle is too high. He feels worried. He can't think what to do. So he just stays there. That makes it easy to take his picture.

The hamster is in someone's hands. He is happy there while his picture is taken. You could put a hamster in the middle of a table, too, and set a feast in front of him. Watch him through the camera. He'll settle down to eat. When he picks up a piece of food, take his picture.

Chapter Four
A Beginning and an End

Babies

You got your rodent when he was a baby. When he is seven to nine weeks old, he is grown up. If you have a female, she can be a mother. A male must mate with your female to start the babies growing.

Buy a male rodent and a separate cage for him to live in. Put your female into the male's cage. He will like her to visit his home, but she might not want him in her home. If you don't want to buy another rodent, let your female visit a friend's male in his cage for a few days. A female hamster does not like a strange male hamster. She may try to fight him. Watch for a few minutes. Take her out of the male's cage if she attacks him. Try again the next day.

Soon the male begins to follow the female around. He holds her around her middle. He is trying to mate. Your female might act annoyed and squeak at him. But when her body feels it is the right time to start babies, she will mate.

Put the female back in her own cage in three

Left: Newborn rodents have no hair. Their eyes are shut tight and their ears are stuck to their heads. These babies are rats.
Right: By the end of the first week, the baby rats begin to grow hair.

days. Get vitamin drops from the pet store to add to her water. The directions on the bottle tell you how much to put in. Give your pet snacks of cheese, vegetables, and meat, too. The growing babies need these extra vitamins and foods.

Give the mother soft materials for her nest. Her babies grow inside her for only two to three weeks. Then they are born in the nest, usually at night.

When all her babies are born, the mother lets them suck milk from the nipples on her belly. Keep giving her vitamins and snacks. She must make a lot of milk now. Sometimes a baby wanders away from the nest. The mother carries him back in her mouth.

You can watch the babies grow and change. The mother will not usually mind if you peek into the nest once a day. But be careful the first time you try it. Some mother rodents do bite. The mother will not like you to touch the babies yet. Wait until they come out of the nest by themselves when they are three or four weeks old. Don't clean the cage until then either.

The babies can leave their mother as soon as she stops feeding them milk. Her cage will be getting crowded by then. You can't keep so many babies. If your friends don't want them, a pet store can find homes for them.

Left: A three-week-old rat beginning to open his eyes. He is still much smaller than his mother.
Right: A baby rat taking his first walk away from the nest. He is four weeks old.

Rodent Troubles

Pet rodents may escape from their cages. Whenever you put your pet in his cage, close the door right away. Some rodents can push the top off a cage, and cats can open tops, too. If you have a tank cage or cake-pan cage, put a book or a rock on it to hold the top down.

Pet rodents may run away when you are playing with them, too. If you have a cat, shut him out of the room. Play with your pet on a table or on the floor in the middle of a room. Your toys or his toys can be near you, but every other part of the floor should be bare. Rodents don't like to run across bare places.

You may see your pet happily playing on the floor. You are sure he will stay there. You go away to do something else. When you come back, your pet is gone. Did he run away because he doesn't love you? No. He ran away because he is a rodent. Rodents run, and rodents hide. They can't help it.

A rat will usually come back. He is more curious and less frightened than other rodents. But a mouse, a hamster, or a gerbil may not come back. He feels confused. His cage and nest have been his home. Now he can't find his house. He is too scared to come out to look for it.

Rodents don't go very far to hide. Your pet is probably still in the same room where he disappeared. Get a plastic container or a coffee can to catch him in. Get a piece of cardboard for a lid. Slowly and quietly look for your pet. Pick each thing up off the floor to see if he is hiding under it. Look under furniture and under pillows. Look inside closets. Look in drawers, and behind books or toys that are on shelves.

If you see your pet, don't grab him. Grabbing scares him. He might bite. Offer him your hand to climb on. He may climb right into it. But if he runs away, watch where he goes. Then use the coffee can. Put the can on top of your pet. Slide the cardboard under the can. Turn the can and cardboard over together. Your pet will fall to the bottom of the can. Then you can pick him up and put him back into his cage.

If you don't find your pet the day he escapes, get a Havaheart trap from a hardware store or friend. Read the instructions that come with it. Put peanut butter and seeds in the trap. Set the trap at night in the same room where your pet escaped. Put it near a hiding place—by a radiator or under a sink. Sometimes you can find out where a pet rodent is hiding. He chews on things at night. If you listen carefully, you can hear him. Then you will know where to put the trap.

Your pet gets hungry. He smells the food and goes into the trap. The door closes, but he is not hurt. The trap is like a small cage.

A Havaheart trap

A Sick Pet

One day you might notice that something is wrong with your pet. He looks skinny. He has lost some of his hair. He moves slowly, or he trembles.

When something looks wrong with your pet, call the pet store or an animal doctor. Tell them what you notice. They may know what to do if your pet is hurt. They may know what medicine will help his sickness. Or they may tell you to feed your pet different foods and to put vitamin drops in his water bottle. Sometimes pet stores and animal doctors don't know what to do about a sick rodent. Then there is very little you can do for your pet.

Rodents often get sick because they need more vitamins. Vitamin drops help. Follow the directions on the bottle. Be sure you are giving enough snacks. Give your pet bones to chew on. Give him cheese. Give him raw spinach, carrots, and apples. Give him raw hamburger, too. He will choose the snacks his body needs to make him better.

Sometimes no good foods or medicines can make your pet better. He is too hurt. He is too sick. Or he is too old. It is time for him to die.

Every animal has to die one day. Dying is always sad. You will feel better if you give your dead pet a funeral. You could put his body inside his own nest. Or you could wrap him in a soft piece of cloth. Dig a hole in the ground to put him into. Your pet would have liked that dark soft earth. Say what you feel like saying. Say how soft your pet was, or how nosy, or how much you miss holding him in your hands. Put earth over his body. You could put a stone on his grave, or plant a flower there. Then you can come to see his grave, until you don't feel sad anymore.

Index